AN ODYSSEY IN LIGHT AND SHADOW OF
CULLINAN'S AURA

KRITHUJA K V

An Odyssey in Light and Shadow of Cullinan's Aura © 2024 Krithuja K V

All Rights Reserved

Made with Notion Press Platform
www.notionpress.com

"To the unseen architects of my journey, the quiet forces that thread strength into my light and shadow. To my family, friends, and the ethereal spirits who dwell in the unspoken spaces of my words. You are the steady compass guiding my steps, the silent rhythm behind every verse. This collection is a testament to the love, presence, and unwavering support that shapes my essence."

PREFACE

Life mirrors the brilliance of the Cullinan diamond, a marvel of contrasts where light and shadow converge, strength meets grace, and every facet reveals an untold narrative. An Odyssey in Light and Shadow of Cullinan is a poetic tapestry woven from the intricate interplay of nature's rhythm, the boundless cosmos, and the silent connections that tether us to one another and the universe. Each verse embodies the essence of life's dynamic dance resilience entwined with vulnerability, stillness merging with motion, and light discovering its purpose within the tender embrace of shadows.This collection transcends the realm of words, offering an invitation to delve into the profound harmony of opposites, the quiet potency of the unseen, and the enduring beauty found in life's ephemeral yet transformative moments. Through these poems, I hope to guide you toward a deeper appreciation of life's exquisite dualities, where fleeting instances carry timeless significance, and contrasts unify to craft a narrative as timeless as the cosmos itself.

ACKNOWLEDGEMENT

This book is a culmination of countless moments, people, and Inspirations that have shaped my life and this collection of poems. I am profoundly grateful to those who stood by me and believed in my vision, even when the path seemed unclear. To my family, your unconditional love and steadfast encouragement have been my anchor and guiding light. You have been my greatest supporters, and I dedicate this milestone to you.

To my ride-or-die friends, you guys are the real MVP's always hyping me up and standing by my side no matter what. Thank you for being my sounding boards, cheerleaders, and constant source of joy. Your unwavering support, endless laughter, and shared adventures make every moment brighter. I'm beyond grateful for your kindness, your loyalty, and the way you show up for me, time and again. Here's to many more memories, laughter, and moments that remind me how lucky I am to have you all!

I also wish to thank the universe for its quiet symphony nature, with its breathtaking beauty; the cosmos, with its mysteries; and life, with its intricate dance of light and shadow. These have been my muses, igniting the spark within me to create.

A gem that embodies the delicate interplay of light and shadow in every thought, Whose unspoken wisdom weaves through the words I've inscribed. In the tranquility of shared moments, these pages unfurl, And within them, the essence of this journey is exquisitely etched, living on in quiet reflection ties...

The Flame of Cullinan

A spark ignites, unseen yet bright,
A flame that glimmers in the night.
It flickers with a tender grace,
A quiet glow, a sacred space.
Through shadows deep,
it finds its way,
Guiding hearts that lost their sway.
In whispers soft, it speaks of time,
Of strength, of bonds,
of paths that climb.
Cullinan's fire, steadfast and true,
A timeless glow, forever new.
It weaves a thread of hope and light,
A silent rhythm in the heart's twilight.
Through every storm,
it holds its flame,
A beacon steady, without name.
A constant guide, of boundless hue,
Cullinan's spark, the world's own cue.

In the Shadows

Beneath the moon's soft gaze, we linger,
Hands clasped, a promise through our fingers.
Shadows stretch, but they do not scare,
For in their silence, we are aware.
Though unseen, the bond remains strong,
In every step, we are meant to be.
The world may darken, but we find a way,
In the quiet, the truth will stay.

A walk in the garden

In the garden, where colors bloom,
We walk in peace, amid the quiet gloom.
Each petal's fall a fleeting memory,
Yet in each moment, a quiet plea.
The breeze hums a song of old,
While in the earth, stories are told.
Among the flowers, we pause, we breathe,
In the stillness, we find reprieve.

The Starry Horizon

The horizon stretches far and wide,
A line where dreams and starlight collide.
The stars above, a distant guide,
Whispering tales where secrets hide.
In their twinkling, a silent plea,
A reach towards the vast, endless sea.
We wander beneath the cosmic sky,
Wondering what keeps us from flying high.

Through the Storm

Through the storm, we hold our ground,
The winds howl, but we make no sound.
The rain may fall, the night may break,
But we find strength with each step we take.
No shelter, yet we feel no fear,
For in the chaos, we're always near.
Through the fury, a calm is born,
A quiet strength in hearts reborn.

The Silent Sea

The sea is vast, its depths unknown,
In its silence, we are grown.
Beneath the surface, currents swirl,
Where whispered thoughts are left to twirl.
In the stillness, there's room to breathe,
To let go of what we cannot keep.
The sea, though silent, speaks of time,
A rhythm untouched, so pure, so prime.

Whispers in the Breeze

The breeze carries whispers through the trees,
Of fleeting moments, soft as these.
It tells a story, old and true,
Of connections born out of view.
In its touch, there's a secret told,
Of quiet bonds that cannot unfold.
In the rustle, a song is sung,
Of all the things we've yet to become.

In the quiet hours

In the quiet hours, we find our peace,
Where all the noise of life may cease.
No words are spoken, yet we know,
In the stillness, we let it go.
The weight of the world fades from view,
As we linger here together,
amidst only our presence.
In silence, we find our way,
Through the night and into the day.

The Cosmic Dance

The stars move, the universe turns,
In every twist, the heart yearns.
The cosmic dance, so vast, so free,
Yet in its pulse, I hear you and me.
Through galaxies wide, we seek and find,
The rhythm that binds, the ties that unwind.
In the silent sway of endless space,
There's a trace of your familiar face.

The Unseen Path

There's a path unseen, beyond the known,
A journey where the seeds are sown.
With every step, the road reveals,
The quiet strength that each heart feels.
No map, no guide, yet here we stand,
Our hearts a compass, hand in hand.
In the unknown, we walk unafraid,
For the road is ours to make, unswayed.

Beneath the moonlight

The moonlight bathes us in its glow,
A gentle light, it's something
that resonates with us.
In its quiet, we share our thoughts,
In the soft embrace, nothing is lost.
Though no words are needed, we understand,
The world stops as we take our stand.
In the stillness, something speaks,
Of dreams, of hopes, of futures unique.

In the Garden of Time

The garden grows, through seasons hand,
Time weaves its threads across the land.
Petals fall, yet we remain,
Through shifting winds, we break no chain.
The earth beneath, so still, so wise,
Reminds us that nothing ever dies.
In the garden, time has its way,
Yet in each moment, we choose to stay.

Beyond the Horizon

Beyond the horizon, the world is vast,
A place where memories slowly pass.
We reach for what we cannot see,
Yet in that longing, we are free.
The horizon beckons, but we stand still,
For in this moment, we are fulfilled.
Though the future calls with a distant sound,
Together, we'll find our way, unbound.

A Dance of Souls

We move as one, though we stand apart,
In every step, we leave a mark.
A dance so quiet, so pure, so true,
In each motion, we're reborn anew.
No rhythm known, yet we find our way,
A bond that speaks, though words may stray.
In the dance, we lose ourselves,
Yet find each other, time and time again.

The still Waters

The still waters reflect the sky,
A mirror of the world gone by.
Beneath the calm, the depths are deep,
Where dreams are planted, and secrets sleep.
In their silence, we find our place,
A quiet moment, a soft embrace.
The waters speak of what is real,
In their stillness, our hearts heal.

Between the Stars

Between the stars, there's space to roam,
A place where we may find our home.
In the silence of the cosmic dance,
We seek the rhythm, we take the chance.
The stars whisper, but never tell,
Of stories lived and secrets held.
Between them, we exist, just so,
In the vast unknown, we let it flow.

The Lasting Flame

The flame flickers, but does not die,
A light that burns beneath the sky.
Through the years, it remains aglow,
A steady presence in the ebb and flow.
Though winds may blow and shadows cast,
The flame endures, steadfast and vast.
In its glow, a warmth is found,
A quiet force that knows no bound.
Its gentle dance, a timeless song,
A beacon bright, where spirits belong.
Through trials faced and battles fought,
The flame reminds of lessons taught.
Its glow reflects a bond so pure,
A strength within, steadfast and sure.
No storm can quench, no dark can claim,
The undying power of its flame.

"In the heart of this odyssey, Cullinan's brilliance casts its aura unseen yet everpresent, a guiding light through shadows. May this journey speak to the gems who carry such quiet radiance in their lives."